Generative AI with Microsoft Azure – Practical

Handbook

Contents

Part I: Introduction to Generative AI and Microsoft Azure

Chapter 1: Introduction to Generative AI

What is Generative AI?

Generative AI refers to a subset of artificial intelligence focused on creating new content, such as images, text, music, and more, that is often indistinguishable from content created by humans. Unlike traditional AI models that focus on recognizing patterns and making predictions, generative AI models learn the underlying distribution of data to generate new instances from that learned distribution.

Generative AI is made possible by advancements in deep learning, particularly through the development of complex neural networks that can capture intricate data patterns. These models have revolutionized various fields by enabling machines to create realistic and high-quality content autonomously.

Applications and Use Cases

Generative AI has a wide array of applications across different industries, including:

- **Art and Design**: Artists and designers use generative AI to create unique artworks, graphic designs, and animations. Tools powered by AI can generate new design concepts, suggest color palettes, and even create entire pieces of art.

- **Healthcare**: In healthcare, generative AI can be used to generate synthetic medical data for research, simulate medical images for training purposes, and even assist in drug discovery by creating new molecular structures.

- **Finance**: The finance industry leverages generative AI for tasks like algorithmic trading, where AI can generate and test new trading strategies, and for fraud detection by creating realistic fraudulent transaction scenarios for model training.

- **Entertainment**: In the entertainment sector, generative AI is used for creating realistic video game graphics, generating new music compositions, and producing special effects in movies.

- **Natural Language Processing (NLP)**: AI models can generate human-like text for chatbots, virtual assistants, and content creation, providing more natural and engaging interactions.

Overview of Generative Models

There are several key types of generative models that have driven the progress in generative AI:

- **Generative Adversarial Networks (GANs)**: GANs consist of two neural networks, a generator and a discriminator, that are trained together. The generator creates new data instances, while the discriminator evaluates their authenticity. This adversarial process leads to the generation of highly realistic data.

- **Variational Autoencoders (VAEs)**: VAEs are a type of autoencoder that learns to encode input data into a latent space and then decode it back to recreate the input. This latent space representation allows for the generation of new data by sampling and decoding from this space.

- **Transformers**: Transformers are a type of neural network architecture particularly effective in processing sequences of data, such as text. They have revolutionized NLP by enabling models like GPT (Generative Pre-trained Transformer) and

BERT (Bidirectional Encoder Representations from Transformers) to generate coherent and contextually relevant text.

Chapter 2: Getting Started with Microsoft Azure

Introduction to Microsoft Azure

Microsoft Azure is a cloud computing platform and service created by Microsoft. It provides a comprehensive suite of cloud services, including those for computing, analytics, storage, and networking. Azure supports a wide variety of programming languages, tools, and frameworks, making it a versatile choice for developing and deploying applications.

Azure's cloud services are categorized into various domains, such as AI and machine learning, databases, DevOps, and security. For those interested in generative AI, Azure offers a robust ecosystem that includes Azure Machine Learning, Cognitive Services, and specialized AI infrastructure.

Setting Up Your Azure Account

To get started with Azure, you need to create an Azure account. Here's a step-by-step guide:

1. **Visit the Azure Website**: Go to the Microsoft Azure homepage (azure.microsoft.com) and click on the "Start free" button.

2. **Sign Up or Sign In**: If you already have a Microsoft account, you can sign in. Otherwise, sign up for a new account.

3. **Provide Billing Information**: Enter your billing information. Azure offers a free tier with credits that you can use to explore the services.

4. **Verify Your Identity**: Microsoft may ask for identity verification through a phone number or credit card.

5. **Access the Azure Portal**: Once your account is set up, you can access the Azure Portal, the

web-based interface for managing all Azure services.

Azure AI and Machine Learning Services Overview

Azure provides a comprehensive suite of AI and machine learning services designed to empower developers and data scientists:

- **Azure Machine Learning**: This service allows you to build, train, and deploy machine learning models. It supports popular frameworks such as TensorFlow, PyTorch, and scikit-learn.

- **Azure Cognitive Services**: These are pre-built APIs for vision, speech, language, and decision-making tasks. They enable developers to integrate advanced AI capabilities into their

applications without deep AI expertise.

- **Azure Databricks**: An analytics platform

  optimized for Azure, providing a fast, easy, and

  collaborative Apache Spark-based analytics

  service. It's ideal for big data processing and

  machine learning.

Chapter 3: Azure Machine Learning Studio

Navigating the Azure ML Studio Interface

Azure Machine Learning Studio is an integrated, end-to-end data science and advanced analytics solution. Here's how to navigate its interface:

1. **Home Dashboard**: The dashboard provides an overview of your resources, recent projects, and quick links to create new resources.

2. **Workspace**: The central hub where you manage experiments, datasets, models, and other resources.

3. **Designer**: A drag-and-drop interface for building machine learning pipelines without coding.

4. **Notebooks**: An integrated Jupyter notebook environment for writing and running Python code.

5. **Automated ML**: A tool for automatically building and tuning machine learning models.

Creating and Managing ML Workspaces

A workspace in Azure Machine Learning is a central place to manage all the resources and assets related to your machine learning projects. Here's how to create and manage workspaces:

1. **Creating a Workspace**:

   - Go to the Azure Portal.

- Click on "Create a resource" and search for "Machine Learning".

- Click on "Machine Learning" and then "Create".

- Fill in the required details such as workspace name, subscription, resource group, and region.

- Click "Review + create" and then "Create".

2. **Managing Workspaces**:

- Navigate to your Machine Learning workspace in the Azure Portal.

- Use the left-hand menu to manage resources such as datasets, experiments, models, and endpoints.

- Monitor the status of your experiments and deployments from the workspace dashboard.

Key Features and Capabilities

Azure Machine Learning Studio offers a range of powerful features to streamline the development and deployment of machine learning models:

- **Experimentation**: Track and manage your experiments, including metrics and outputs.

- **Model Management**: Register, organize, and version your models for easy retrieval and deployment.

- **Pipelines**: Automate your machine learning workflows by creating pipelines that orchestrate the steps in your process.

- **Deployment**: Deploy models as RESTful web services or batch scoring services, and manage the deployed endpoints.

- **Monitoring and Logging**: Monitor the performance and health of your models in production, with built-in logging and diagnostic tools.

- **Collaboration**: Share workspaces and resources with team members, enabling collaborative development and experimentation.

By understanding these foundational elements, you'll be well-equipped to harness the power of generative AI using Microsoft Azure's comprehensive suite of tools and services.

Provide content in human form for Part II: Generative Models on Azure Implementing GANs on Azure Understanding Generative Adversarial Networks Setting Up a GAN Project in Azure Training and Evaluating GANs with Azure ML Variational Autoencoders (VAEs) on Azure Introduction to VAEs Building and Deploying VAEs in Azure Use Cases and Applications Transformers and Language Models on Azure Overview of Transformer Architecture Implementing Language Models (e.g., GPT, BERT) in Azure Fine-Tuning and Deployment

Part II: Generative Models on Azure

Chapter 4: Implementing GANs on Azure

Understanding Generative Adversarial Networks

Generative Adversarial Networks (GANs) are a class of machine learning frameworks designed by Ian Goodfellow and his colleagues in 2014. GANs consist of two neural networks: the generator and the discriminator. These two networks are trained simultaneously in a process where the generator creates data that the discriminator evaluates.

- **Generator**: This network generates new data instances. Its goal is to produce data that is indistinguishable from real data.

- **Discriminator**: This network evaluates the data produced by the generator and tries to distinguish between real and generated data. Its goal is to accurately classify data as either real or fake.

During training, the generator and discriminator engage in a zero-sum game where the generator tries to produce better fake data to fool the discriminator, while the discriminator improves its ability to detect fakes. This adversarial process continues until the generator produces highly realistic data.

Setting Up a GAN Project in Azure

To set up a GAN project in Azure, follow these steps:

1. **Create an Azure Machine Learning Workspace**:

   - Go to the Azure Portal.

   - Search for "Machine Learning" and select "Create".

   - Provide the necessary details like workspace name, subscription, and resource group.

   - Click "Review + create" and then "Create".

2. **Set Up a Compute Instance**:

- In your Machine Learning workspace, go to "Compute" > "Compute instances".

- Click on "New" to create a new compute instance.

- Choose an appropriate VM size with GPU support, such as NC series for deep learning tasks.

- Configure the instance and click "Create".

3. **Launch Jupyter Notebooks**:

- Once the compute instance is running, go to the "Notebooks" section in your workspace.

- Create a new Jupyter notebook or import an existing one to start developing your GAN.

Training and Evaluating GANs with Azure ML

To train and evaluate GANs using Azure Machine Learning, follow these steps:

1. **Prepare the Data**:

   - Load and preprocess your training data. For image-based GANs, ensure the images are resized and normalized.

2. **Build the GAN Architecture**:

- Define the generator and discriminator models using a deep learning framework such as TensorFlow or PyTorch.

- Compile the models with appropriate loss functions and optimizers.

3. **Train the GAN**:

  - Implement the training loop where the generator and discriminator are trained alternately.

  - Track the training progress and losses using Azure ML's logging and monitoring tools.

4. **Evaluate the GAN**:

- Generate new samples using the trained generator.

- Evaluate the quality of the generated samples using qualitative (visual inspection) and quantitative (inception score, Frechet Inception Distance) methods.

5. **Save and Register the Model**:

- Save the trained generator model.

- Register the model in the Azure ML workspace for easy retrieval and deployment.

Chapter 5: Variational Autoencoders (VAEs) on Azure

Introduction to VAEs

Variational Autoencoders (VAEs) are a type of generative model that learns a probabilistic representation of the input data. VAEs consist of an encoder, a decoder, and a latent space. The encoder maps input data to a distribution in the latent space, and the decoder reconstructs the data from this distribution.

- **Encoder**: Compresses the input data into a latent space representation, typically as a mean and variance.

- **Latent Space**: Represents the compressed data distribution, allowing for sampling and generating new data instances.

- **Decoder**: Reconstructs the input data from the sampled points in the latent space.

VAEs are particularly useful for generating new data samples that are similar to the training data and for tasks such as image denoising and anomaly detection.

Building and Deploying VAEs in Azure

To build and deploy a VAE in Azure, follow these steps:

1. **Set Up the Workspace and Compute**:

   - Use the same steps as described for setting up a GAN project to create a workspace and a compute instance.

2. **Build the VAE Architecture**:

- Define the encoder and decoder networks using a deep learning framework.

- Implement the reparameterization trick to sample from the latent space during training.

- Compile the VAE with appropriate loss functions, typically combining reconstruction loss and KL divergence.

3. **Train the VAE**:

- Load and preprocess the training data.

- Train the VAE, monitoring the reconstruction and KL divergence losses.

- Use Azure ML's experiment tracking to log the training metrics.

4. **Evaluate the VAE**:

   - Generate new samples by sampling from the latent space and passing them through the decoder.

   - Evaluate the quality of the reconstructed and generated samples.

5. **Deploy the VAE**:

   - Save the trained VAE model.

   - Use Azure ML to deploy the model as a web service for real-time inference or batch processing.

Use Cases and Applications

VAEs have various applications, including:

- **Image Generation and Reconstruction**: Creating new images or reconstructing corrupted images.

- **Data Compression**: Compressing data into a lower-dimensional latent space for storage and transmission.

- **Anomaly Detection**: Identifying anomalies by comparing reconstruction errors.

- **Text Generation**: Generating coherent text sequences in natural language processing tasks.

Chapter 6: Transformers and Language Models on Azure

Overview of Transformer Architecture

Transformers are a type of neural network architecture designed for handling sequential data. They have become the foundation for many state-of-the-art models in natural language processing (NLP). The key components of transformer architecture include:

- **Self-Attention Mechanism**: Allows the model to weigh the importance of different words in a sequence, capturing long-range dependencies.

- **Encoder-Decoder Structure**: Encodes the input sequence into a set of continuous representations and decodes them into an output sequence.

- **Positional Encoding**: Adds information about the position of words in the sequence, enabling the model to understand the order.

Notable transformer models include GPT (Generative Pre-trained Transformer), BERT (Bidirectional Encoder Representations from Transformers), and their variants.

Implementing Language Models (e.g., GPT, BERT) in Azure

To implement language models like GPT or BERT in Azure, follow these steps:

1. **Set Up the Workspace and Compute**:

   - Create a Machine Learning workspace and a compute instance with sufficient GPU resources.

2. **Prepare the Data**:

   - Load and preprocess text data for training. For fine-tuning, use domain-specific datasets.

3. **Choose a Pre-trained Model**:

   - Use pre-trained models available in frameworks like Hugging Face Transformers. These models can be fine-tuned for specific tasks.

4. **Fine-Tune the Model**:

   - Load the pre-trained model and prepare it for fine-tuning.

   - Train the model on your dataset, adjusting hyperparameters for optimal performance.

   - Use Azure ML's logging and monitoring tools to track the fine-tuning process.

Fine-Tuning and Deployment

To fine-tune and deploy a transformer model, follow these steps:

1. **Fine-Tuning**:

   - Fine-tune the pre-trained model on your specific dataset.

   - Monitor training metrics and evaluate the model's performance on a validation set.

2. **Save and Register the Model**:

   - Save the fine-tuned model and register it in the Azure ML workspace.

3. **Deploy the Model**:

- Use Azure ML to deploy the model as a web service.

- Configure the deployment settings, including the compute resources and scaling options.

4. **Monitor and Manage the Deployment**:

- Monitor the deployed model's performance and usage.

- Use Azure's diagnostic tools to track and resolve any issues.

5. **Update and Retrain**:

- Periodically update and retrain the model with new data to maintain and improve its performance.

By understanding and implementing these generative models using Microsoft Azure, you can leverage the power of advanced AI techniques to create innovative solutions across various domains.

Provide content in human form for Part III: Advanced Topics and Use Cases AI-Powered Image and Video Generation Deep Learning for Image and Video Synthesis Tools and Services in Azure for Media AI Case Studies and Applications Natural Language

Generation (NLG) Techniques for Text Generation

Leveraging Azure Cognitive Services for NLG Real-

World Applications Creating Conversational Agents

with Azure Building Chatbots and Virtual Assistants

Integrating Azure Bot Services and Cognitive Services

Enhancing Conversational AI with Generative Models

Part III: Advanced Topics and Use Cases

Chapter 7: AI-Powered Image and Video Generation

Deep Learning for Image and Video Synthesis

Deep learning has significantly advanced the field of image and video synthesis, enabling the creation of highly realistic and complex visuals. Key techniques include:

- **Generative Adversarial Networks (GANs)**: Used to generate photorealistic images and videos by training a generator and discriminator in an adversarial process.

- **Variational Autoencoders (VAEs)**: Useful for generating new images by learning a latent space representation of the data.

- **Recurrent Neural Networks (RNNs)** and **3D Convolutional Networks**: Applied in video synthesis to capture temporal dependencies and generate coherent sequences of frames.

These models have enabled applications such as deepfake creation, video super-resolution, and style transfer, where the style of one image or video is applied to another.

Tools and Services in Azure for Media AI

Azure offers a variety of tools and services to facilitate media AI tasks, including image and video synthesis:

- **Azure Machine Learning**: Provides a platform for training, deploying, and managing deep learning models. It supports popular frameworks like TensorFlow and PyTorch.

- **Azure Cognitive Services - Computer Vision**: Offers pre-built APIs for image analysis, object detection, and image captioning.

- **Azure Media Services**: Enables the processing, storage, and streaming of video content, with capabilities for encoding, analyzing, and transforming video files.

- **Azure Databricks**: An analytics platform optimized for big data and machine learning tasks, suitable for processing large-scale image and video datasets.

Case Studies and Applications

1. **Deepfake Detection and Creation**:

   - Companies use GANs to create realistic
     video content for entertainment and
     advertising. Conversely, Azure's AI tools
     help in detecting and mitigating the

spread of deepfake videos by analyzing video authenticity.

2. **Video Super-Resolution**:

   - Video streaming services employ deep learning models to enhance video quality by increasing resolution. Azure's scalable infrastructure supports the training and deployment of these models for real-time applications.

3. **Art and Content Creation**:

   - Artists and designers use AI-powered tools to generate new artworks, combining styles and creating novel visual experiences. Azure Machine Learning and Cognitive Services provide the necessary tools to build these creative applications.

Chapter 8: Natural Language Generation (NLG)

Techniques for Text Generation

Natural Language Generation (NLG) involves creating human-like text from data using various techniques:

- **Recurrent Neural Networks (RNNs) and Long Short-Term Memory (LSTM) Networks**: These models capture temporal dependencies in sequences, making them suitable for generating coherent text.

- **Transformers**: Advanced models like GPT (Generative Pre-trained Transformer) and BERT (Bidirectional Encoder Representations from Transformers) have revolutionized NLG with their ability to understand context and generate high-quality text.

- **Markov Chains**: A simpler statistical approach that generates text based on the probability of word sequences.

These techniques are used for a variety of tasks, including machine translation, summarization, and conversational agents.

Leveraging Azure Cognitive Services for NLG

Azure Cognitive Services provides several tools for NLG tasks:

- **Text Analytics API**: Analyzes text to extract insights, such as sentiment, key phrases, and language detection.

- **Language Understanding (LUIS)**: Helps build natural language understanding into apps, bots, and IoT devices, allowing for intent recognition and entity extraction.

- **Azure OpenAI Service**: Provides access to powerful language models like GPT-3, enabling developers to build advanced text generation applications with minimal effort.

Real-World Applications

1. **Content Creation**:

- Automated content generation for news articles, blog posts, and product descriptions. Businesses use Azure's NLG capabilities to generate large volumes of high-quality text content efficiently.

2. **Customer Support**:

   - Virtual assistants and chatbots use NLG to provide instant, coherent responses to customer inquiries. Azure Bot Services and LUIS facilitate the development of these intelligent agents.

3. **Data-to-Text**:

   - Transforming structured data into natural language reports, such as financial summaries or medical reports. Azure's machine learning tools help create models that translate complex data into readable narratives.

Chapter 9: Creating Conversational Agents with Azure

Building Chatbots and Virtual Assistants

Building effective chatbots and virtual assistants involves several key steps:

1. **Define the Purpose**:

- Clearly outline the goals and tasks the chatbot will handle, such as customer service, information retrieval, or booking appointments.

2. **Design Conversations**:

   - Create conversation flows and design intents and responses that guide user interactions.

3. **Develop the Bot**:

   - Use tools like Azure Bot Service to create, test, and deploy your chatbot. Integrate natural language understanding using LUIS to enable the bot to interpret user inputs accurately.

4. **Integrate with Channels**:

   - Deploy the chatbot across multiple channels, such as websites, messaging apps, and social media platforms, using Azure's channel integration features.

Integrating Azure Bot Services and Cognitive Services

Azure Bot Services, combined with Cognitive Services, provides a robust platform for building and deploying conversational agents:

- **Azure Bot Service**: Offers a comprehensive framework for developing, testing, and managing chatbots. It supports multiple channels and provides tools for continuous deployment and monitoring.

- **Language Understanding (LUIS)**: Integrates with Azure Bot Service to enhance the chatbot's ability to understand and process natural language inputs.

- **QnA Maker**: Allows the creation of a knowledge base from existing content, enabling the chatbot to provide accurate and quick answers to frequently asked questions.

Enhancing Conversational AI with Generative Models

Generative models, such as GPT-3, can significantly enhance the capabilities of conversational agents:

1. **Contextual Understanding**:

   - Use transformer models to provide more

     natural and contextually relevant

     responses, improving the user experience.

2. **Personalization**:

   - Tailor responses based on user

     preferences and past interactions.

     Generative models can generate

     personalized content that resonates with

     individual users.

3. **Dynamic Content Generation**:

   - Create dynamic responses for complex

     queries, enabling the chatbot to handle a

wider range of topics and provide more

detailed information.

4. **Continuous Learning**:

- Implement feedback loops where the

    chatbot learns from user interactions and

    improves over time. Azure's machine

    learning infrastructure supports

    continuous training and deployment of

    updated models.

By mastering these advanced topics and leveraging

Azure's powerful tools and services, you can create

innovative AI-powered solutions that push the boundaries of what's possible in image and video generation, natural language processing, and conversational AI.

Provide content in human form for Part IV: Deployment and Scaling Deploying Generative AI Models on Azure Best Practices for Model Deployment Using Azure Kubernetes Service (AKS) Monitoring and Managing Deployed Models Scaling Generative AI Solutions Scaling Techniques and Strategies Leveraging Azure's Infrastructure for Scalability Cost Management and Optimization

Part IV: Deployment and Scaling

Chapter 10: Deploying Generative AI Models on Azure

Best Practices for Model Deployment

Deploying generative AI models effectively involves several best practices to ensure performance, reliability, and scalability:

1. **Model Optimization**:

   - Optimize your model for inference by using techniques like quantization, pruning, and model distillation to reduce size and improve speed without sacrificing accuracy.

2. **Containerization**:

   - Package your model and its dependencies into a container using Docker. This ensures consistency across different environments and simplifies the deployment process.

3. **Version Control**:

- Implement version control for your models to track changes and manage different iterations. Azure Machine Learning provides tools to register, version, and manage models.

4. **CI/CD Pipelines**:

- Set up continuous integration and continuous deployment (CI/CD) pipelines to automate the process of testing and deploying models. Azure DevOps can help streamline these workflows.

5. **Security**:

- Secure your deployment by implementing authentication and authorization mechanisms. Use Azure Active Directory to manage access and permissions.

Using Azure Kubernetes Service (AKS)

Azure Kubernetes Service (AKS) provides a robust platform for deploying and managing containerized applications, including AI models. Here's how to leverage AKS for deploying generative AI models:

1. **Set Up AKS Cluster**:

   - Go to the Azure Portal, search for AKS, and create a new Kubernetes cluster. Configure the cluster settings, such as node count, VM size, and networking options.

2. **Deploy Containers**:

- Build Docker images of your generative AI models and push them to Azure Container Registry (ACR). Deploy these containers to your AKS cluster using Kubernetes deployment manifests.

3. **Load Balancing**:

- Use Kubernetes services to expose your model deployments and set up load balancing to distribute traffic evenly across replicas. This ensures high availability and scalability.

4. **Autoscaling**:

- Configure horizontal pod autoscaling (HPA) to automatically adjust the number of replicas based on CPU/memory usage or custom metrics. This helps in handling varying loads efficiently.

5. **Monitoring and Logging**:

- Use Azure Monitor and Azure Log Analytics to track the performance and health of your deployed models. Set up alerts to notify you of any issues that require attention.

Monitoring and Managing Deployed Models

Effective monitoring and management of deployed models are crucial for maintaining performance and reliability:

1. **Performance Metrics**:

    - Monitor key metrics such as latency, throughput, and resource utilization. Azure Monitor provides dashboards and alerts to keep track of these metrics.

2. **Model Drift Detection**:

    - Implement mechanisms to detect model drift, where the model's performance degrades over time due to changes in the data distribution. Retrain and update models as needed.

3. **Logging and Debugging**:

   - Enable detailed logging to capture inference requests and responses. Use Azure Log Analytics to analyze logs and diagnose issues.

4. **A/B Testing**:

   - Deploy multiple versions of a model and perform A/B testing to compare their performance. This helps in selecting the best model for production use.

5. **Rollback Mechanisms**:

- Implement rollback mechanisms to revert to a previous model version in case the new deployment causes issues. Azure DevOps and Kubernetes facilitate smooth rollbacks.

Chapter 11: Scaling Generative AI Solutions

Scaling Techniques and Strategies

Scaling generative AI solutions involves various techniques and strategies to handle increased demand and ensure robust performance:

1. **Horizontal Scaling**:

   - Add more instances of your model to handle increased load. Use AKS to manage and scale containerized applications seamlessly.

2. **Vertical Scaling**:

   - Increase the computational power of existing instances by upgrading the VM sizes. This can be useful for resource-intensive models.

3. **Distributed Training**:

   - For large models and datasets, use distributed training across multiple GPUs or nodes. Azure Machine Learning supports distributed training using frameworks like Horovod and PyTorch Lightning.

4. **Batch Processing**:

   - Implement batch processing for large volumes of inference requests. Azure Batch allows you to run large-scale parallel and high-performance computing applications efficiently.

5. **Edge Deployment**:

   - Deploy models to edge devices for real-time inference closer to where the data is generated. Azure IoT Edge facilitates deploying containerized applications to edge devices.

Leveraging Azure's Infrastructure for Scalability

Azure provides a comprehensive set of tools and services to support the scalability of generative AI solutions:

1. **Azure Machine Learning**:

- Use Azure ML for managing the end-to-end machine learning lifecycle, including experimentation, model training, and deployment at scale.

2. **Azure Kubernetes Service (AKS)**:

   - Utilize AKS for scalable and resilient deployment of containerized applications. AKS handles orchestration, scaling, and management of containerized applications.

3. **Azure Functions**:

   - Implement serverless computing with Azure Functions to scale your application automatically based on demand. This is particularly useful for event-driven workloads.

4. **Azure Databricks**:

- Leverage Azure Databricks for big data processing and machine learning at scale. It integrates with Azure ML and supports distributed training and data processing.

5. **Azure Front Door**:

- Use Azure Front Door to optimize the performance and availability of your global applications by providing fast, reliable, and secure content delivery.

Cost Management and Optimization

Managing and optimizing costs is essential when scaling AI solutions. Here are some strategies:

1. **Right-Sizing Resources**:

   - Choose the appropriate VM sizes and instance types based on workload requirements. Avoid over-provisioning resources.

2. **Spot Instances**:

   - Use Azure Spot Virtual Machines for cost-effective compute options for non-critical workloads. Spot VMs can significantly reduce costs compared to standard VMs.

3. **Autoscaling**:

   - Implement autoscaling to adjust resources dynamically based on demand. This ensures you only pay for what you use.

4. **Cost Monitoring**:

   - Use Azure Cost Management and Billing to monitor and analyze your spending. Set up budgets and alerts to keep track of costs.

5. **Optimize Storage**:

   - Choose the right storage options based on access patterns. Use Azure Blob Storage for cost-effective storage of large datasets and leverage Azure Disk Storage for high-performance needs.

By following these practices and leveraging Azure's robust infrastructure, you can effectively deploy, scale, and manage generative AI models to meet the demands of modern applications while optimizing performance and costs.

Part V: Case Studies and Future Trends

Chapter 12: Industry Case Studies

Generative AI in Healthcare

Generative AI is transforming healthcare by enabling advanced diagnostic tools, personalized treatment plans, and efficient data management. Key

applications include:

1. **Medical Imaging**:

   - **GANs for Image Enhancement**: GANs are

     used to enhance the quality of medical

     images, such as MRIs and CT scans,

     providing clearer visuals for diagnosis. For

     instance, GANs can reduce noise and

     improve resolution, helping radiologists

     identify abnormalities more accurately.

   - **Automated Image Analysis**: Generative

     models assist in segmenting and analyzing

     medical images, identifying regions of

interest, and detecting diseases at an early stage.

2. **Drug Discovery**:

- **Molecule Generation**: Generative models, including VAEs and GANs, are used to design new molecules with desired properties. This accelerates the drug discovery process by predicting the efficacy and toxicity of potential compounds.

- **Virtual Screening**: AI-driven virtual screening of chemical libraries helps in identifying promising drug candidates, reducing the time and cost associated with traditional drug discovery methods.

3. **Personalized Medicine**:

- **Treatment Optimization**: Generative AI models analyze patient data to develop personalized treatment plans, predicting how patients will respond to different therapies. This helps in tailoring treatments to individual needs, improving outcomes.

Applications in Finance

In the finance sector, generative AI enhances decision-

making, fraud detection, and customer experience:

1. **Financial Forecasting**:

   - **Market Predictions**: Generative models are used to predict market trends and stock prices by analyzing historical data and identifying patterns. This helps traders and financial analysts make informed decisions.

   - **Risk Management**: AI models assess and predict risks associated with investments, providing insights into potential market fluctuations and enabling better risk mitigation strategies.

2. **Fraud Detection**:

- **Anomaly Detection**: Generative AI identifies unusual patterns in transaction data, flagging potentially fraudulent activities. By continuously learning from data, these models improve their detection accuracy over time.

- **Synthetic Data Generation**: AI generates synthetic transaction data to train and test fraud detection systems, enhancing their ability to recognize new types of fraud without compromising sensitive customer information.

3. **Customer Service**:

- **Chatbots and Virtual Assistants**: Financial institutions deploy AI-powered chatbots to handle customer inquiries, provide financial advice, and assist with transactions, improving customer satisfaction and operational efficiency.

- **Personalized Recommendations**: Generative models analyze customer behavior and preferences to offer personalized financial products and services, enhancing the customer experience.

Generative AI is revolutionizing creative industries by automating content creation and enhancing artistic endeavors:

1. **Digital Art and Design**:

   - **AI-Generated Artwork**: Artists use generative models to create unique artworks, exploring new styles and forms that blend human creativity with machine intelligence. AI tools like GANs can generate paintings, sculptures, and digital installations.

- **Design Assistance**: AI aids designers by generating multiple design variations, optimizing layouts, and suggesting color schemes, thereby streamlining the creative process.

2. **Music Composition**:

- **Automated Music Generation**: AI models compose original music pieces by learning from existing compositions. These models can create background scores for films, video games, and advertisements, catering to specific moods and themes.

- **Collaborative Tools**: Musicians use AI tools to experiment with new sounds and collaborate on compositions, pushing the boundaries of musical innovation.

3. **Content Creation**:

- **Text Generation**: Generative AI models like GPT-3 create written content, including articles, stories, and scripts. These models assist writers by generating ideas, drafting content, and even completing entire narratives.

- **Video Production**: AI tools enhance video production by generating special effects, animating characters, and editing footage. This reduces production time and costs while expanding creative possibilities.

Building Advanced Generative AI Models with Microsoft Azure

Generative AI is transforming industries by enabling applications that range from content creation to sophisticated automation. Microsoft Azure provides an ecosystem tailored to building, deploying, and managing these generative models at scale. This chapter dives into advanced techniques for developing generative AI models using Azure's AI platform, focusing on optimizing architectures, leveraging pre-trained models, and ensuring scalability for enterprise applications.

Leverage Azure Machine Learning for Generative AI Development

Azure Machine Learning (Azure ML) is a cornerstone for creating generative AI models. It provides tools for model development, including training large-scale transformer architectures like GPT or T5. Advanced users can optimize these models using distributed training and advanced data pipelines.

One of the essential strategies involves fine-tuning pre-trained generative models available through the Azure OpenAI Service. These models can be adapted to domain-specific tasks by retraining them with curated datasets. For instance, consider a healthcare organization creating a generative model to summarize patient records. By fine-tuning GPT-4 via Azure ML pipelines, developers can achieve a high degree of domain-specific accuracy while reducing the overall training time and costs.

Building Custom Architectures on Azure

Azure supports custom generative AI architectures using its scalable compute and storage options. Developers can use Azure ML to define multi-modal models that combine text, image, and even video data for applications like automated video captioning or creative content generation.

A practical example involves training a multi-modal model to generate marketing collateral, such as banner designs paired with persuasive ad copy. By leveraging Azure's NC-series virtual machines with NVIDIA GPUs, this task can be scaled efficiently. Developers can further employ the Azure Cognitive Toolkit (CNTK) for implementing custom attention mechanisms, improving model creativity and coherence.

Scaling Generative AI with Azure Kubernetes Service (AKS)

Azure Kubernetes Service is critical for managing the deployment of large-scale generative AI models. AKS supports advanced orchestration, allowing enterprises to scale up their inference workloads dynamically. Imagine a retail company deploying a generative chatbot for Black Friday sales. Using AKS and Azure's

Horizontal Pod Autoscaler, the chatbot can handle

thousands of concurrent customer interactions,

ensuring seamless user experience during peak traffic.

Azure's MLflow integration helps with model

versioning and lifecycle management in these scalable

deployments. Developers can experiment with various

model versions and maintain a robust CI/CD pipeline

to ensure frequent updates without service downtime.

Generative AI Optimization Techniques on Microsoft

Azure

As generative AI models grow in complexity,

optimizing them for performance and cost becomes

paramount. This chapter explores advanced optimization strategies tailored to the Azure ecosystem, ensuring that generative AI deployments are both efficient and impactful.

Optimizing Training Pipelines with Azure Databricks

Azure Databricks offers an excellent platform for creating efficient training pipelines. By integrating with Delta Lake, developers can preprocess large datasets and feed them into models without compromising on quality or speed. Delta Lake's ACID-compliant architecture ensures reliable and repeatable experiments.

Consider a company building a generative AI model for legal document summarization. Azure Databricks can be used to perform tokenization, text normalization, and embeddings generation at scale. With MLlib, developers can incorporate distributed gradient descent algorithms, significantly reducing training time while maintaining accuracy.

Accelerating Inference with Azure Inferencing Tools

Inference optimization is vital for generative AI applications, especially those requiring real-time responses. Azure provides hardware-accelerated options such as FPGA-based inference using Azure Percept or GPU acceleration via Azure NCv4 VMs. These tools enable near-instantaneous generation of outputs like personalized recommendations or dynamic content creation.

Developers can integrate Azure Cognitive Services with pre-trained models to enable faster deployments without compromising on model fidelity. For example, a customer service chatbot powered by Azure OpenAI can utilize Cognitive Services for sentiment analysis, improving its contextual responses.

Reducing Costs with Spot VMs and Reserved Instances

Cost management is a significant challenge in generative AI projects. Azure Spot VMs offer a cost-effective solution for non-critical workloads, such as model retraining and experimentation. Reserved Instances, on the other hand, provide consistent savings for production-level deployments.

By combining Spot VMs with Azure's Machine Learning Pipelines, developers can schedule cost-sensitive tasks during off-peak hours. For example, a media company generating movie scripts can reserve GPUs for inference while using Spot VMs for offline text generation experiments, achieving substantial cost reductions.

Ethical AI and Bias Mitigation in Azure-Based Generative Models

Building generative AI models comes with ethical responsibilities, particularly around bias mitigation and ensuring transparency. This chapter delves into advanced practices for addressing these challenges within the Azure ecosystem.

Using Azure Responsible AI Dashboard

The Azure Responsible AI Dashboard is an advanced toolset designed to identify and mitigate biases in AI models. For generative AI, this means evaluating the outputs of models like GPT-4 for fairness across different demographics or content categories. The dashboard's Explainability and Fairness modules provide insights into how a model arrived at a particular output, enabling developers to pinpoint and rectify issues.

Consider a generative AI model designed for news summarization. By using the dashboard, developers can detect if the model exhibits bias toward specific topics or regions, ensuring that the summarizations remain objective and inclusive.

Implementing Differential Privacy with Azure Confidential Computing

Azure Confidential Computing provides the framework for implementing differential privacy in generative AI models. By adding noise to training data, developers can ensure that sensitive information is protected without compromising model utility. This technique is particularly relevant for healthcare and financial sectors, where privacy concerns are paramount.

For example, a fintech company training a generative model on transaction data can leverage Azure Confidential Computing to anonymize data effectively. This ensures compliance with regulations like GDPR while maintaining the accuracy of predictions and generated outputs.

Monitoring and Maintaining Transparency in Generative AI Deployments

Azure Monitor and Log Analytics play a pivotal role in tracking model behavior in production. By setting up custom telemetry, developers can gain real-time insights into how the model interacts with users and whether it adheres to ethical guidelines.

Imagine a creative writing tool generating essays.
Azure Monitor can track the diversity of topics and
styles generated, ensuring the model does not
perpetuate stereotypes or generate offensive content.
Log Analytics provides historical data, enabling
retrospective evaluations and continuous
improvement.

Advanced Fine-Tuning of Generative AI Models on Microsoft Azure

Fine-tuning is a critical process for tailoring generative
AI models to specific domains or tasks. Azure offers a
suite of tools and services to enable sophisticated
fine-tuning workflows, making it possible to achieve

high accuracy and efficiency in domain-specific applications. This chapter focuses on advanced techniques for fine-tuning using Azure resources.

Domain-Specific Fine-Tuning with Azure OpenAI Service

Azure OpenAI Service simplifies the fine-tuning of large pre-trained models like GPT-4 for specialized applications. By uploading proprietary datasets, organizations can teach models to generate highly relevant outputs. For instance, a pharmaceutical company can fine-tune a language model on clinical trial data to create a system capable of drafting detailed medical reports.

The key to successful domain-specific fine-tuning lies in the quality of data preprocessing. Azure Databricks can be employed to clean, normalize, and tokenize input data, ensuring compatibility with Azure OpenAI's training requirements. Leveraging Azure Blob Storage for dataset storage allows seamless integration with the fine-tuning pipeline, making the process efficient and scalable.

Few-Shot and Zero-Shot Fine-Tuning

Few-shot and zero-shot techniques are gaining traction for applications requiring minimal labeled data. Azure ML's integration with transformers supports these methods by enabling transfer learning on massive pre-trained models. Few-shot fine-tuning allows organizations to adapt a model with just a handful of examples, which is particularly useful in dynamic industries where data is scarce.

For example, an e-commerce platform can fine-tune a model with a few product descriptions to generate engaging marketing content for newly launched products. Using Azure Compute Instances with distributed training, developers can complete these fine-tuning tasks faster while ensuring high performance.

Implementing Active Learning Loops

Azure ML Pipelines can be used to implement active learning loops, where the model identifies ambiguous outputs and requests additional labeled data. This iterative approach ensures that the model continuously improves its understanding of domain-specific nuances.

An insurance company could deploy an active learning pipeline to enhance its policy recommendation system. By monitoring uncertain outputs, the system prompts human agents to provide additional training data, thereby refining the model's ability to draft personalized policy suggestions.

Multi-Modal Generative AI Applications with Azure

The future of generative AI lies in multi-modal models that can process and generate data across multiple types of input, such as text, images, and audio.

Microsoft Azure provides the infrastructure and tools

necessary to build and deploy multi-modal AI systems.

This chapter delves into advanced techniques for

creating multi-modal applications, highlighting their

versatility and potential.

Designing Multi-Modal Architectures

Azure supports multi-modal model design through

frameworks like PyTorch and TensorFlow, which are

natively compatible with Azure ML. Developers can

combine transformer-based models with

convolutional or recurrent neural networks to create

systems capable of processing diverse inputs.

For example, a news aggregation platform can use a multi-modal model to analyze text articles, generate summaries, and pair them with relevant images. By leveraging Azure's NC-series VMs equipped with powerful GPUs, the platform can process and infer from vast datasets in real-time.

Integrating Vision-Language Models

Azure OpenAI Service provides access to cutting-edge vision-language models, enabling the development of applications like visual storytelling or automated video captioning. These models can be fine-tuned using datasets stored in Azure Data Lake, making it easier to manage large-scale projects.

An entertainment company might use Azure to create a system that generates movie trailers by analyzing scripts, selecting relevant scenes, and producing promotional content. Azure Batch can further streamline video processing tasks, ensuring efficient scaling for large production workloads.

Creating Audio-Enhanced Generative Systems

With Azure Cognitive Services, developers can integrate audio processing capabilities into generative models. Text-to-speech (TTS) and speech-to-text (STT) APIs enable the development of applications like voice-enabled virtual assistants or audio content generators.

For instance, a podcast creation tool can utilize Azure TTS to generate voiceovers for script-based podcasts. By combining TTS with Azure ML, the tool can even adapt the tone and pitch of generated audio to match the desired emotional impact.

Federated Learning for Generative AI on Azure

Federated learning is an advanced technique that enables AI models to be trained across distributed datasets while preserving data privacy. Azure's infrastructure supports federated learning for generative AI, making it a powerful tool for organizations handling sensitive information.

Federated Model Training with Azure ML

Azure ML provides the framework for implementing federated learning workflows. Organizations can use Azure Kubernetes Service (AKS) to orchestrate distributed training across multiple devices or locations. This approach allows data to remain decentralized while contributing to a global model.

Consider a healthcare consortium training a generative model for diagnostic image synthesis. Federated learning allows hospitals to train the model using local datasets without sharing sensitive patient information. Azure's Confidential Computing and Differential Privacy capabilities further ensure data security during the training process.

Implementing Secure Aggregation Protocols

Federated learning relies on secure aggregation protocols to combine local updates into a global model. Azure provides tools like Azure Key Vault for managing cryptographic keys, ensuring the security of aggregated updates.

A financial institution might use federated learning to train a fraud detection model across its regional branches. By encrypting updates from each branch, the institution can build a robust model while maintaining compliance with data privacy regulations.

Optimizing Federated Inference Workflows

Once a federated model is trained, Azure ML Pipelines can be used to deploy it for distributed inference. This allows organizations to deliver AI services locally while benefiting from the collective knowledge of the global model.

For example, a retail chain can deploy a federated generative model to recommend store layouts based on regional sales patterns. Each store receives localized recommendations while contributing insights to improve the global model's accuracy.

Chapter 13: Future Trends in Generative AI

Emerging Technologies and Innovations

The field of generative AI is rapidly evolving, with several emerging technologies and innovations set to shape its future:

1. **Advanced Neural Architectures**:

   - **Transformers and Beyond**: New neural architectures, building on the success of transformers, continue to push the boundaries of what generative models can achieve. Research into more efficient and powerful architectures promises even greater capabilities.

2. **Hybrid Models**:

- **Combining Approaches**: Hybrid models that combine the strengths of different generative techniques, such as GANs and VAEs, are emerging. These models leverage the advantages of each approach to generate higher-quality outputs.

3. **Federated Learning**:

- **Decentralized Training**: Federated learning enables AI models to be trained across multiple decentralized devices while maintaining data privacy. This approach is particularly relevant in sectors like healthcare and finance, where data sensitivity is paramount.

Ethical Considerations and Responsible AI

As generative AI becomes more prevalent, addressing ethical considerations and promoting responsible AI practices are crucial:

1. **Bias and Fairness**:

   - **Mitigating Bias**: AI models must be trained on diverse datasets to avoid perpetuating biases. Ensuring fairness and transparency in AI decision-making processes is essential to build trust and inclusivity.

2. **Privacy and Security**:

- **Data Protection**: Protecting user data and ensuring privacy is paramount. Techniques like differential privacy and secure multi-party computation help safeguard sensitive information while enabling AI training and deployment.

3. **Regulation and Governance**:

- **Ethical Guidelines**: Developing and adhering to ethical guidelines and regulations is necessary to ensure responsible AI usage. Policymakers, researchers, and industry leaders must collaborate to create frameworks that balance innovation with ethical considerations.

The Future of Generative AI on Azure

Microsoft Azure is poised to play a significant role in the future of generative AI, providing a robust platform for innovation and deployment:

1. **Enhanced AI Services**:

   - **Continued Development**: Azure will continue to expand its suite of AI services, offering more advanced tools and capabilities for developers and businesses. This includes improvements in model training, deployment, and management.

2. **Integration with Emerging Technologies**:

- **AI and Quantum Computing**: Azure's integration with emerging technologies like quantum computing promises to unlock new possibilities for generative AI, enabling the development of more powerful and efficient models.

3. **Sustainability and Efficiency**:

- **Green AI Initiatives**: Azure is committed to sustainability, focusing on reducing the environmental impact of AI workloads. Advances in energy-efficient AI models and data center operations will contribute

to greener AI practices.

4. **Collaborative Ecosystem**:

- **Partnerships and Community**: Azure

  fosters a collaborative ecosystem,

  encouraging partnerships with academic

  institutions, research organizations, and

  industry leaders. This collaborative

  approach accelerates innovation and the

  adoption of generative AI technologies.

www.ingramcontent.com/pod-product-compliance
Lightning Source LLC
La Vergne TN
LVHW051659050326
832903LV00032B/3900